ONE DAY WE MET THE LIONS ...

SIX DAYS OF FUN

JANET MACKENZIE

CHRISTIAN FOCUS PUBLICATIONS

Contents

A Word to Children

A Word to Parents

Published by:
Christian Focus Publications Ltd.
Geanies House, Fearn, Ross-shire,
IV20 1TW, Great Britain.

A WORD TO CHILDREN

Do you like to spend time with your friends and family? Rachael, James and Peter do. They love to go out together, and like nothing more than to hear a Bible story from Mum or Dad afterwards.

Rachael, James and Peter are learning that God should play a very important part in our lives. They know that he loves us and is interested in every one of us. You can enjoy learning about the Bible just like the three children as you read their adventures. Just turn over the page!

THE ZOO

Do you like school holidays? Rachael, James and Peter do. They were going to spend a day at the zoo with their cousins and were very excited.

What a crowd the families made as they met together! Of course, even with a guide book it was hard to decide where to go first.

'Can we see the monkeys?' suggested Elizabeth.

'I want to see lions,' said James.

'How about an ice cream?' said Peter.

At last they agreed to see as many animals as possible.

There were zebras, tall, elegant giraffes and dangerous looking crocodiles. They laughed at pelicans with their funny beaks, and watched an elephant having a bath. The enormous snakes were only fed on Fridays. What a shame it wasn't today.

So they watched sea-lions jumping up to catch fish instead.

After lunch, they saw night animals like bats and bush babies.

Then it was time for an ice cream. The families sat down near the lions' enclosure and felt glad that the fierce big cats were behind tough glass windows.

At last it was time to say good-bye to the cousins. What a wonderful day it had been, and they talked about their favourite animals all the way home.

'I liked the baby elephant,' said Rachael. 'He was really cute!'

'Shall we read about some lions tonight?' Mum suggested, turning to Daniel chapter 6. The children agreed, and heard about Daniel who was thrown into the lions' den because he refused to stop praying to God.

King Darius did not want Daniel to be killed, and said, 'May your God rescue you.' God sent an angel to shut the mouths of the lions, and Daniel's life was saved.

The children remembered those well-fed lions and their rows of sharp teeth.

They prayed that God would give them a strong faith like Daniel, and asked him to help them always.

SNAKES

Have you ever been to the zoo? James, Rachael and Peter enjoyed their visit so much that they often spoke about it. James had taken photos of their favourite animals, and they enjoyed reading about them in a souvenir guide book.

'Look at this,' exclaimed James, who was reading about the reptile house. 'Do you remember those enormous snakes we saw? Some, like the python and the boa constrictor, coil themselves around their prey and crush them until they suffocate. Others poison their victims by injecting them with venom from their fangs!' He enjoyed giving the others all the gory details! 'A bite from a black mamba can kill you in under one hour.'

'Ugh! That's awful,' gasped Rachael. 'It would take longer than that to get to hospital!'

'Actually, they keep some anti-dotes for treating some types of snake bites at the zoo,' James added, and they all gave a sigh of relief.

The Reptile House

'Do you remember what the people of Israel had to do if they were bitten by the snakes in the desert?' asked Dad, who had been listening to the conversation. They listened as he read from Numbers chapter 21.

The people of Israel were complaining bitterly about their long journey through the wilderness, so God sent snakes into the camp and many people were bitten and died.

God told Moses to make a brass snake and put it on a pole. Anyone who had been poisoned by the venom had only to look at it to be saved.

Dad turned in the Bible to John chapter 3, where Jesus said to Nicodemus that, just as the people of Israel had to look to the brass snake to be cured, so we must look to the death of Jesus on the cross to save us from our sins.

The children prayed, thanking God for what they had learned, and asking him to help them to put their trust in him every day.

BONFIRE NIGHT

It was a lovely starlit evening. The children had rushed through their homework and now stood outside in the still, cold air. They had been looking forward to the bonfire all day. As a special treat, Rachael, James and Peter were being allowed out late and they were eager to go. They were waiting for mum to take them.

'Come on, Mum,' called Rachael. 'They're lighting the bonfire at seven.'

They could see people making their way towards the bonfire. Other mums and dads were taking their children to see the bonfire. Some of the parents carried fireworks. The children looked forward to seeing the bright colours they would make.

It wasn't long before they were pushing through the crowd to see the enormous bonfire.

Then the firework display began and

they watched as rockets shot high into the air, sending down showers of beautiful sparks. Catherine wheels whirled, and sprays of different coloured stars lit up the night sky. The children shouted 'Ooh's' and 'Aah's' of delight until the last firework had flickered out and the bonfire had died down to a pile of glowing embers.

'That was great,' said Peter, as they walked home.

'What a heat from the bonfire!' James remembered. 'I wouldn't like to go any closer.'

Rachael made a face. 'My hair smells of smoke!'

Back at home, Mum made hot chocolate, and they sat warming their hands on the mugs as Mum read them a Bible story.

'This is about a very hot fire,' Mum said, turning to Daniel chapter 3. The children listened thoughtfully as she read about the three friends who refused to worship the golden statue. King Nebuchadnezzar was very angry and ordered his men to make a furnace seven times hotter than usual. Shadrach, Meshach and Abednego were thrown into the flames.

James reminded them that he had singed his hair when helping his uncle burn straw on the farm, but not a hair on these mens' heads had been damaged. When they read that not even the smell of the fire was on them, they remembered what Rachael had said about her hair. Most of all, they noticed that the three friends had been prepared to obey God even if it meant they would die.

The family bowed their heads. They thanked God for what they had learned, and asked for the help to obey him always.

SNOW

James opened a bleary eye one winter morning and looked around the room. Everything seemed so bright. A car went past outside. Why did it sound so quiet and slow? He leapt out of bed and rushed to the window. 'Snow!' he gasped, pulling back the curtains. 'Peter wake up!'

All sleepiness disappeared as Peter scrambled to join him.

'It looks like a picture, doesn't it?' whispered Peter.

'And look at the sky. It's

pink and glowing as the sun rises.' Rachael had heard the commotion and came to join her brothers at the window.

'Quick!' said James. 'Let's get dressed and go outside.'

They raced downstairs in their warm coats gloves and hats. What fun they had! They ran around the garden making the first footprints in the fresh white snow, then followed the track left by a rabbit until it disappeared under the fence.

Snowballs flew, and laughing merrily, they ducked and dodged to escape.

'Time for breakfast,' Mum called, and the three rushed indoors, their cheeks rosy with cold.

At school that day the children made an enormous snowman and gave it a scarf. Then everyone took turns to slide down a sloping part of the playground. 'What a day!' they agreed, returning home on the school bus that afternoon.

After supper, Dad opened the Bible at Psalm 51. When they came to verse seven where David asks God to 'wash me and I shall be whiter than snow,' they understood what he meant. The family remembered how pure and white it was, and they talked about God taking away all the wrong things they had done. They asked him to forgive them for all the hurtful things they had said and for all the bad thoughts. They were thankful to know that God could make them whiter than the snow which they had enjoyed so much.

FLOODS

It rained and it rained. The children went to bed listening to the pitter-patter of drops against the window and the gurgle in the drain pipes. It was still pouring the next morning when they awoke and the sky was very dark indeed.

'Put on your wellington boots today,' Mum reminded, before they left to catch the school bus. They set off, laughing and splashing in the puddles on the way.

'Mum, Mum, you should have seen the flooding up by Gavin's house!' The children burst in from school, flinging off wet coats and boots.

'Yes,' said Peter, 'and the water was halfway up the bus wheels.'

'The river is almost up to the top of its banks,' Rachael reported.

'We even saw some sheep on a bit of high ground surrounded by water,' said James, panting for breath.

That evening the news-reader warned drivers to take great care as many roads were flooded. The children watched as cars drove along the road, spraying up water on either side!

Can you guess which Bible story the family had for their prayer time that night? Yes, they read in Genesis chapter 7 about Noah, who was warned by God that there would be a flood. Noah was to build a boat which would save his family and the animals.

Rachael, James and Peter had watched the rain for two days, but in Noah's time, it didn't stop for forty days and nights. The water covered the mountain tops, but the family were safe in the ark because they believed and trusted God. Mum reminded them that we must believe God like Noah, and put our trust in Jesus who will keep us safe.

Before they went to sleep, the children thanked God for giving them Jesus, and asked that he would keep them safe always. Will you be like Noah, and trust God too?

THE PICNIC

It was Saturday; the sun was shining, and the family had found a lovely spot by the river for a picnic. Mum lay reading a book, while Rachael found smooth pebbles and made them skim across the top of the water. James and Peter played football with Dad.

'Don't kick it too hard, James,' Dad called. Too late! The ball went flying past Peter and landed with a splash in the middle of the fast-flowing water.

'Oh no!' James shouted. 'It will be washed right away to the sea.'

'Not if we're quick,' replied Peter who pulled off his shoes and sped into the icy water. What a speed it was moving at!

'We didn't bring a towel. We weren't intending going in for a dip!' laughed Mum as Peter waded back triumphantly with the ball.

'I don't mind. The sun will dry my feet,' said Peter. 'Anyway, I'm very hungry. When is it time to eat?'

'Right now. Come on everyone!'

They watched the river flow by as they ate their lunch, and Dad spoke.

'Can you imagine what it was like for the Israelites when they crossed the River Jordan on dry ground? Shall we read that story tonight?'

So, when the family sat down to read the Bible that evening, Dad read Joshua chapter 3. The children imagined what it must have been like for the people of Israel to step out across the river bed, while the water built up like a wall beside them.

Verse ten says, 'This is how you will know that the living God is among you.' That certainly was an amazing sign to show that God was with them, wasn't it?

As they prayed, the family thanked God for his wonderful world, and for his power over everything. They asked for the help to believe him just as the people of Israel had done when they stepped out in faith and crossed the dry river bed.

A WORD TO PARENTS

How do you teach children to enjoy the Bible and help them to apply its teachings to their own experience and understanding? We hope you will agree that this book achieves the objective by using short stories about events which will be familiar to many children. Each story is drawn from the author's own personal experience, and concludes with a Biblical perspective which is naturally introduced into the narrative.

This book is designed to be read by children on their own, or with a parent or Sunday School teacher, and each story can be used as a basis for further discussion and Bible study. We trust that the book will be an inspiration for Christians, and that it will provide useful ideas for future devotional times with young ones.